Tease
the
Monkeys

A guide to non-buttheaded management

By

Christian L. Holz

3rd edition – June 2023

TABLE OF CONTENTS

INTRODUCTION

When friends ask me how I like my job, I reply, "Imagine working for a boss who's not a butthead."

More than half the time, this thought completely staggers them. They stare off into space and can't seem to grasp the concept. So that started me thinking about what characteristics of "boss behavior" separated the buttheads from the non-buttheads.

This is a collection of observations and sayings collected over too many years of working for both types of boss, and also sometimes being the boss. I can't claim that these are entirely original, or unique, or maybe even historically accurate: I'm pretty sure that I enhance and embellish the stories each time I tell them so that they might be more exaggeration than anything. Please try to find – maybe even embrace – the underlying message in the stories without focusing on the details

Chapter One
TEASE THE MONKEYS

I did some volunteer work with a Boy Scout troop and was invited to sit on an Eagle Scout candidate's review board. In the conference room was a whiteboard, and someone had carefully written the following on the whiteboard:

Tease the monkeys all you want, but don't mess with the gorilla. – Tarzan, 1928

The more that I thought about it, the more that spoke to organizational politics. You can look at an organizational chart, but it does not tell you much about the real relationships within a company or a club or a government unit or a community. The persons with the actual power – the gorillas – are not always evident until you work with everyone for a while.

For all you know, the receptionist who you ignored when you came in for an interview is actually the sister of the company president. And that's a fairly tame example of the kind of relationship that might exist without your knowledge. My buddy Dean passed along some wisdom from his father that I'll paraphrase here:

Son, as you go through life, you'll be presented with hundreds of opportunities to keep your mouth shut. Seize every one of them!

– Pa Bull

You can probably come up with one or two (or twenty!) times when you have put your foot in your mouth and gave it a good twist. Here's just one of mine.

On the phone with a woman at a competitor's company, we were exchanging ideas on how to prepare some government paperwork. She asked me what I thought about the method that had been given to us by another person – a man at a third company. I said that I didn't think very highly of it. She asked me to elaborate and I said that I thought he wasn't the expert that he held himself out to be, that he was probably making a lot of money consulting with that flawed method, and while we're at it, he had a bad haircut too – or something like that.

Guess what two people left their respective spouses to marry each other soon after that conversation?

You may never figure out who's a monkey and who's a gorilla. The safest bet is to assume that they're all gorillas.

Chapter 2
SOME MANAGEMENT BASICS

Managing is a continuous process, a cycle of three things:

- Planning

- Execution

- Control or feedback

I guess I should clarify that this defines *effective* management. Too many people in positions of management – as opposed to people who are actual managers – fail the third step, control or feedback, which is:

1. Examine the results of your plan and execution and see whether it had the desired results, then

2. Use that information to make your future plans.

Somewhere along the cycle, we hope that the very first plan was based on something other than SWAG ("scientific wild-ass guess") but that's not always the case. Here's another story.

The boss called me and said that I should get two more phone lines installed. Since I'm cheap – I mean, trying to protect the organization's cash flow – I asked him why to do that. He said that he was getting complaints that the phones weren't being answered. I tried to get more specific information out of him but all I was doing was making him angry that I was questioning his order. Okay, fine, I ordered two more lines to add to the ten we already had.

There are at least two things that could have caused the complaints. One is that the phone was ringing but no one was picking it up. That seemed unlikely because we had a full-time receptionist. The other is that all ten lines were already busy so the caller would have heard a busy signal.

That seemed reasonable because there were about fifty employees using those ten lines and receiving transferred calls.

Two more lines made no difference. Complaints continued and I was looking at adding even more lines. Then I happened to go past the reception desk at 9:45 a.m. – break time. I could see that all twelve lines were flashing as if they were ringing but there was no sound. The receptionist was working her crossword puzzle and ignoring the flashing lights.

Like an idiot, I asked if there was something wrong with the phone panel since there was no ringing. Her reply was, "No, I turned the ringer off. I'm on break and I can't work my puzzle with all that noise."

I swear, I am not making this story up. And by the way, she was a gorilla and not a monkey. She had family connections to the extent that she ended up taking my boss's job when he resigned.

As for the phones, the company went from not answering ten lines to not answering twelve lines, and now you know why. Planning and executing without control is not management. It's just … filling a chair with a warm body.

Chapter 3
FUNDAMENTAL FAILURE TO MANAGE

Fundamental Failure to Manage, FFM for short. If all you're going to do is plan and execute with no regard for whether your plan had the desired results, then you might as well not even plan: just execute, execute, execute.

Take a look at most laws at any level of government. Most are an attempt to solve some problem. But *almost none of them* include a measurement process, a metric to determine whether the law had the intended effect or actually made the problem worse. And even fewer laws have a built-in "sunset" tied to the measureable to void the law if it is ineffective.

Instead, the lawmakers create another law.

Here is a quote attributed to Thomas Paine but probably from twentieth century anarchist Edward Abbey:

The duty of a patriot is to

protect a country from its government.

Those who work in government might consider their obligation to try to minimize the extent to which the governed need protection from their government. Plan, execute *and* control. If something doesn't work, quit doing it.

"DO THE RIGHT THING" IS NOT THE SAME AS "DO THE THING RIGHT"

Non-profits and governments are often led by people who say that their objective is to "do the right thing". They hold themselves out as caring individuals – and I won't dispute that until they prove me wrong – who try to use the organization's resources to have positive effects on their target clientele.

A social service agency may have a stated objective of improving the lives of people in the community by assuring that clean affordable housing is available, that utilities like electricity and water are widely distributed and affordable, and that health care is accessible. Maybe there is a program that helps pay utility bills if a community member comes up short one month, and to "do the right thing" is to pay their bill.

Without regard to whether taking responsibility for someone's utility bill for a month actually helps them – that's an entirely different debate – the fact is that someone within the agency needs to perform certain precise steps to get that bill actually paid. This is the person or persons who "do the thing right". At the minimum, they get a copy of the bill, write a check, get it delivered to the utility company on time, and maintain the records to show that they did not steal the money for themselves.

Chapter 4
JUST GET IT DONE

Many of us have experienced situations where we were told to "just get it done" by bosses who had no clue whatever about the amount of actual work required in doing the thing right.

But I would still rather do it myself and know that it's done right, and here's why:

If you don't have time to do it right,

how will you ever find time to fix it?

It is provable that fixing something always takes longer than it would have taken to do it right in the first place. If that was not true, then the "fixing-it" method would be the standard procedure.

Unfortunately, acquiring a reputation as the person who does the thing right has a side effect:

Do a job twice and it's yours.

Now you can take that as a problem or an opportunity. You can build a career in almost any field as the person who does the thing right. In fact, I'd much rather hire someone who has a reputation of doing the thing right than someone who always "does the right thing" or worse yet, someone who knows what to do but doesn't bother to do it.

On the other hand …

One of my favorite lunchtime activities is reading the comics. Thanks to the internet, I'm not limited to the dozen or so comics that might be in the local dead-tree news. On my list is "Arlo and Janis" by Jimmy Johnson. Several years ago, Mr. Johnson wrote this great strip.

Arlo was looking out at the yard, and he called out to his son:

Arlo: Gene, I thought I asked you to mow the yard.

Gene: I did!

Arlo: Son, if a job is worth doing, it's worth doing right.

Gene: It wasn't worth doing.

There may be some things we do day after day in our jobs that just aren't worth doing. It may not be your place to evaluate that, but try not to impose duties that are not worth doing on those who you supervise. If you don't think that such things exist, maybe you should ask.

Here are just a couple examples. One place where I was consulting had the receptionist creating a printed list every day of all incoming mail. The list was not saved or turned into a searchable database, which maybe – maybe – would have justified the effort. The list was turned over to the supervisor and filed in a drawer. I couldn't help myself: I had to know why this was being done. According to the receptionist, someone months ago had claimed that they sent some important paperwork to the facility but no one knew what happened to it. So now they logged all incoming mail.

You should know that the list did not indicate what happened to the mail after it was logged: who it went to, whether it was thrown out, or anything else that might be useful. It was just logged and the log was filed.

So the next time that someone says they sent some important paperwork, and it's not on the log, what can you say with certainty? Can you say that it was not received? No. You can only say that it's not on any of the logs. It's always possible that the item was received but the receptionist failed to put it on the log.

Trying not to sound like I thought the whole thing was as ridiculous as it certainly was, I had to ask, "How often does anyone ask to look for something on the logs?"

The answer? "No one has ever asked to see the logs yet."

I think I might have found a job that was not worth doing.

As promised, here is another example. This one will mean much more to an accountant but most people who have worked in an office can understand it anyway.

I found a government organization that wrote checks just once a week – not a problem – but they were spending a whole day trying to file the check copies. The controller had set up a filing system where all invoices and attached check copies were filed by vendor (that is, they were sorted alphabetically by the name on the check). Every check-copy and invoice for every check they had ever written was filed this way, no matter how old. This is a very common system, by the way.

Some letters of the alphabet end up with more documents than others. You move files from drawer to drawer to make up for this over time. If you decide to archive old items to some other storage location, someone needs to go through every folder in every drawer to pull the old items. The only good thing is that it's very easy to find documents if you know the vendor's name.

If you're trying to find out how you managed to spend so much on office supplies in the last year, however, you need the help of your computer software. This will give you a list of all the checks written for one expense category including the vendor name and the check number.

Of course, that same software would have let you list all of the payments to one vendor, and that was the excuse for the file-by-vendor filing system. Is spending a whole day filing by vendor starting to look like a job not worth doing?

We switched to filing check-copies in check-number order. That happens to be the way they came off the printer. We still attached the invoices to the check-copies. But when it came time to file them, we picked up the whole stack and took them to the file cabinet. The whole stack was placed behind last week's checks, and the job was done. Elapsed time less than a minute.

You can label the drawers of the cabinets by check number and know that you will never need to change the labels once a drawer is full.

Since check-number order is also chronological order, "archiving" means moving the oldest cabinet.

The drawback? Staff needs to know how to use the computer software. You can laugh, but I encountered one controller who insisted on keeping that by-vendor system because she would not learn how to use the software to get the information she wanted.

In her defense, think of the amount of work involved in switching over to the simpler system. To re-file all existing items would be to put them in check-number order. (Imagine the volume of documents considering that they wrote about a thousand checks per month.) But there could be a cutoff date after which the new system would be used. Then when you looked up a payment on the computer, you'd know whether to look in the old files or the new files.

And that brings up another fine management motto, one commonly called "The Seven P's":

Proper prior planning prevents
pitifully poor performance.

The time to decide how to set up your filing system is before you write your first check. Rather than saying, "This is the way everyone does it," you can see that a little bit of thought could result in a lot of saved time and effort.

Chapter 5
DEALING WITH PEOPLE

Here is something I heard recently:

This would be a great place to work except for the suppliers, the customers and the employees.

Hopefully that was someone's idea of a joke. Unfortunately there may be some truth in that.

There is probably at least one supplier, one customer or one employee who accounts for more "trouble" than all of the rest combined. It might be the supplier who makes you prove that you paid the bills (same supplier, same kind of request several times a year), or the customer who is never satisfied no matter what you do, or the employee who doesn't seem to understand that you just want an honest week's work in exchange for the pay you give.

I was "given" an employee by the boss one time. That is, the boss knew the guy and hired him, then decided that the guy should work in my department. The guy (I'll keep calling him that) was under-skilled, which was bad enough, and he also had bad work habits ranging from failure to bathe to failure to show up for work until two or three hours after schedule. Because of the way that he was hired, he was more of a gorilla than a monkey so I had to work around his issues.

The guy's wife also worked at the same place but in a different department. One morning I was standing near the front door drinking my coffee as starting time approached. The guy came roaring into the driveway and stopped by the door. His wife jumped out, and then he turned the car around and drove away while I watched.

I asked his wife what was up and she said something to the effect of, "He's your problem, not mine." Ohhhh kayyy.

The guy did not return until the next morning, and then he went right to his desk and started work. I couldn't believe that he wasn't even going to say anything, so I asked him:

Me: What was the deal yesterday?

The Guy: Well, didn't you hear how much noise the car was making? I had to go fix the exhaust system.

Me:　　　It took you all day, and you couldn't even call?

The Guy: I figured that if you really needed me, you could come and get me.

You can imagine what I was thinking. I knew I couldn't fire the guy – monkey versus gorilla, you know - but several months later, after the guy failed to call or show three days in a row, I made sure the boss knew about it: job abandonment. That was the end of the guy's employment.

But that was not the end of the story. About six months later, I received a call from a potential employer asking for a reference for the guy.

I couldn't help myself: I laughed into the phone, and then I apologized. The woman on the other end of the line said, "That's okay. He told me you might laugh."

All I could say after that was to ask, "Well, does that tell you what you need to know?" She agreed that it did.

One time I was fortunate not to be the object of a customer's ire. Instead, one of my co-workers was repeatedly tasked with trying to satisfy a person who was determined not to be satisfied. You know what I'm talking about: there are people who just are not "happy" unless they're miserable.

This customer (actually a client at a social service agency) had nothing good to say about the agency, the work we did, the way we did things, or the genetic makeup of anyone who worked there. And she thought she was entitled to special care because she was one of the oldest clients of the agency. Time to throw in another saying:

Wisdom comes with old age,

but sometimes old age arrives alone.

Just because you're old does not mean that you're wise, in other words. In some communities, however, it might make you a gorilla instead of a monkey.

I'll get back to that story shortly, but I want to insert the text from an episode of "Baldo", a daily cartoon by Hector D. Cantu and Carlos Castellanos. Baldo is a teenager working part-time in an auto parts store.

He's trying to deal with an ornery customer (who just happens to be an old man).

Grouch: What's wrong with you? This isn't what I want! Do you know what you're doing? Can you get me a smarter clerk?

Baldo: No, sir, I'm sorry.

Grouch: And why not?

Baldo: The smarter clerk saw you coming and left.

Anyway, after this one client became the focus of the third or fourth staff meeting, the assigned social worker was at her wits' end. She hated to come to work and she was starting to take it out on her fellow workers.

We all talked about the problem and assured the worker that she was doing all that she had the power to do. It was unfortunate, but she was going to need to just smile and follow the rules. All we could offer her was a little printed sign on her bulletin board that she could look at when things were getting her down. It said:

We get pleasure from everyone we deal with: some when they arrive, and some when they depart.

The social worker did not keep working there much longer, but I did note that she took that sign with her.

Chapter 6
THE POST-IT NOTE (registered trademark of 3M)

We use a cash box for the occasional sale at the counter (as opposed to mailed invoices). One of my daily tasks is to count the previous day's cash box, make a bank deposit out of the checks and cash that exceeds the imprest amount, and then move the yellow Post-It note from the outside of the box to the inside of the box. That's how we know that the box has been counted and can now be used again.

One day the Post-It note fell off. It had been used so many times that it just would not stick to the box. I had a pad of blue Post-It notes on my desk, so I replaced the yellow one with a blue one.

It triggered *the end of life as we know it* – at least as far as one of the clerks was concerned. She made a point of calling the new note "stupid" and had to go find a yellow note to replace the blue note. I am not making this up.

I knew better than to invoke a heart attack or a stroke by saying what I really thought, which was the next lesson I'd like to pass along:

Display some adaptability!

If you've "always done it this way", maybe you should take another look at what you're doing.

When you take another look, you might find:

1. There are other ways to do it, and/or

2. It really doesn't matter how you do it, and/or

3. It might not even need doing at all.

After the dust had settled – and I mean several days later! – I suggested that maybe we needed a sign on the wall that said,

"Because that's the way we've always done it"

I'm not claiming to know the better way to do everything. I just think we should consider the possibilities.

Chapter 7
NEVER UNDER-ESTIMATE ANYONE

In the middle of a computer programming assignment, I struggled to find a way to make one of the language's features perform correctly. No matter what I tried, I was unable to get predictable results and I had locked my mind into using this feature to solve a problem that it was not capable of solving.

This was taking place in the back room of a restaurant where I had set up my laptop computer to work through lunch. The head chef, Bob, stopped by and asked, "Having trouble?"

I replied in a very general comment that I could not seem to solve this problem. Bob said something like, "Why don't you run it by me?"

Thinking to myself, sure, a chef is going to understand this – and then, what do I have to lose? So I spelled it out in the least-technical way that I could.

Bob asked me, "Have you thought about approaching it from the direction of [something that was completely different]?"

I thought it over for a few seconds and realized that his approach was much better than mine. In fact, it ultimately solved the problem and gave me some code that I used on a regular basis after that. So what was the deal with Bob?

It turns out that being a chef was Bob's retirement job. He had retired from Honeywell where he was a programmer on mainframe computers practically from their inception.

Lesson learned:

> Never underestimate anyone! You never know from whence you'll get your next great customer, your next great idea, or your next big butt-kicking.

That last part came from karate class, by the way. In martial arts, it is very important that you never underestimate anyone. I doubt that I need to elaborate on that one – but I will.

I was assigned to practice some sparring with a visitor from another club. Holding the rank of black belt, I figured I could take whatever this blue-belt-ranked guy could throw at me. And besides, his seeing-eye dog was sitting over by his gym bag. Seriously.

So I tried to make some sounds with my hands and feet to help the guy figure out where I was. I tapped him on the shoulder lightly a couple of times and he nailed me right in the nose with a great punch.

I backed up and tried a couple more things, throwing a light kick to his midsection. He replied with a solid punch to my midsection that took my breath away.

So I stepped back and asked, "Just exactly how blind are you anyway?" while thinking to myself, if you're not blind I'm going to pound you into the ground in a minute.

He replied that he could make out shapes and light and dark pretty well, and he was seeing my black uniform against the lighter background just fine. I had clearly underestimated him. Our next couple of minutes were on a much more even basis.

Chapter 8
NO SUCH THING AS FOOLPROOF

When writing computer programs, it is important to include ways to handle all possible inputs from the user of the program. That is, the programmer must consider not just the expected inputs but also the *unexpected* inputs.

For example, if you want a user to input the month of their birth, you might want and expect the answers to be a number between 1 and 12. But you need to handle the following situations also:

- if the user leaves it blank

- if the user enters 0 or 13 or 99

– if the user enters the name of the month instead of the number

– if the user enters something meaningless like "XYZ"

This may all seem obvious but a programmer cannot just ignore it. And just when programmers think that they have written a foolproof program, they get bitten by the following bit of truth:

There is no such thing as "foolproof" because fools are so creative.

To put that another way:

You can always find a bigger fool than you had ever expected.

Sometimes the foolish things done by otherwise-normal people make you shake your head in wonder. I was on a consulting engagement as the general manager of a facility that was open around the clock. In the daily paperwork was a shift manager's recommendation to award some paid time off to an employee who had "gone over and above the call of duty" by working extra shifts in a pinch.

This seemed like the kind of behavior that we wanted to reward. One truth of non-buttheaded management is:

Tell your staff when they do something right!

You already take every opportunity to tell them when they do something wrong. A good manager will put at least as much effort into praising and rewarding good behavior as they do in punishing bad behavior.

So I approved the award and asked to be there when the award was to be presented. The shift manager checked the schedule and found that the employee in question had been suspended for three days without pay by the shift manager on the other shift.

I don't know who was right and who was wrong, but I do have a pretty good idea of what that employee thought about management's capabilities in this case.

Bad moves by management can go way beyond foolish. One organization that I knew had about three hundred employees. They recognized longevity of ten, twenty and thirty years with a nice plaque – which was delivered in a plain brown envelope by interoffice mail. And I know of one case where that same envelope included a ten-year plaque and a layoff notice.

I am not making this up. That was extreme buttheaded management.

Organizations like that do not succeed *because* of their management: they succeed *in spite of* their management.

Chapter 9
TRUST THE PEOPLE YOU HIRE

When you hire the right person, you should be able to give them the tools they need and trust them to do the job correctly. "Trust" here has nothing to do with being honest. It's all about giving them credit for some brains and letting them succeed or fail.

Assuming that you hired a person for their skills, you should recognize that it is a reflection on YOU if they fail to meet your expectations. It may not be entirely your fault but you need to own part of it.

If you spend a lot of time looking over someone's shoulder, maybe you should ask whether you failed in your hiring selection. As my buddy Jim puts it:

- Know the way.
- Show the way.
- Get out of the way.

There needs to be a balance between supervising and micro-managing. If you need to put off a scheduled employee evaluation because you don't really know how well your new employee is doing, then your boss should consider that in <u>your</u> next evaluation.

You should know that those scheduled evaluations are incredibly important to your employees. I'll bet that if you asked, they'd tell you that getting feedback is more important to them than the pay increase that often comes with the evaluation.

So here is an example of screwing that up. A co-worker's annual evaluation was at least a month overdue and the boss kept telling the poor guy that he was too busy but whatever he decided would be retroactive to the due date. My co-worker was doing two people's jobs for about six months (salaried, working 60 hours a week with no overtime) because his supervisor had left and not been replaced. When the evaluation was finally done, it was about eight weeks late. My co-worker was given the supervisor position, along with a forty percent (40%!) increase in wages. But the boss didn't make it retroactive as he had promised.

The boss saved about $6,000 by not making the raise retroactive. The employee who had just received a forty percent increase was permanently chapped that the boss had done this. Normally an employee who just got a forty percent increase would do anything you asked. Not in this case. The butt-headed boss, by the way, made $6,000 about every eight days.

When it was announced that the company was being sold, that boss cut his own schedule back from a nice casual 28 hours a week to about 16 hours a week. No change in pay, of course, because the out-of-town owners had no idea what he did or how little he worked. Interestingly, that boss who made it to work before 9:00 a.m. a grand total of ONCE in the four years that I knew of (scheduled 8:00 to 5:00) made a point of commenting on how everyone disappeared right at 5:00, on those rare occasions when he was actually there to witness it.

The lesson and management saying for this:

You can't push a chain. You have to pull it.

This is also from Boy Scout Junior Leader Training. You need to lead your people, be a good example, show how the job is done, and then let your people do their jobs. If you are a bad example, don't be surprised if your people have no respect for you or your initiatives.

Chapter 10
SOME THOUGHTS ON MEETINGS

For a while, I quoted a price for attending meetings that was triple my usual hourly charge. If that tells you what I think about most of the meetings I've ever attended …

There are lots of different reasons that organizations hold meetings. We may have different opinions about the value of meetings so this is where I get to tell you mine.

Sometimes the leadership just wants to announce a new policy or procedure, and the meeting assures that everyone knows about it. It would be less of a waste of time if you'd put it in a memo (which you should probably do anyway so that there's a written record). I'll put this more emphatically:

<blockquote>
If you don't want my input,

cancel the meeting and write a memo.
</blockquote>

Sometimes the leadership wants to get input on possible ways to solve a problem. I think this is a pretty good reason to have a meeting, and it acknowledges the value of the people you've hired. Of course, this can still get screwed up. For example (a real life example), the boss can storm out yelling, "Just fix it!" While you may think you've just been given a blank check to fix it your own way, do you have any doubt that a boss like that would second-guess you? I'll just say that if you're that boss, you're not going to attract and keep good people.

Sometimes the leadership wants to be sure that all managers know what the other managers are doing. On a start-up project, this seems like a good idea to me. It reduces duplicate work and assures that all required tasks are handled by someone.

I'd suggest that these meetings need clear agendas and task-lists, and the time spent in the meetings should not keep those tasks from getting done. If you have to send out for lunch to continue the meeting, you're doing it wrong. (Yes, I've seen that many times.)

Chapter 11
THE SABOTAGE MANUAL

There is a document you can find on the internet titled "Simple Sabotage Field Manual". It was published in 1944 by the Office of Strategic Services, which eventually became the U.S. Central Intelligence Agency (CIA).

The purpose of the manual was to give citizens of the enemy some ways to disrupt the war-making ability of their own countries. But some of these techniques sound familiar with respect to the behavior of buttheaded bosses.

One suggestion is to be pleasant to inefficient workers and give them undeserved promotions, while discriminating against efficient workers and finding fault with their work.

While some bosses might think they're being good "motivators" by promoting workers who don't deserve it, they probably are not considering the effect on their true hard workers who see what is happening. My saying for this is kind of clumsy but here goes:

When you treat your bad help well, you're treating your good help bad.

Another item from the sabotage manual is to refer all matters to committees for further consideration and study. In other words, avoid taking a decision or actually doing anything, and spread the blame as widely as possible.

On a couple of occasions I have worked for bosses who have had absolutely no positive impact on the place they worked. They made it a point to never take a decision on anything and to be absent when anything "interesting" was going on.

They could have been replaced with a coin that you flip heads or tails, and no one would have been any worse off. Plus, in one case, the company would have saved a ton of money because the boss was paid more than the state Governor. For the non-butthead, I suggest:

If you don't take a decision, don't criticize the decision made by someone else.

One more idea from the sabotage manual is to require excessive documentation and multiple levels of signatures before any action can be taken. I will probably upset a lot of people who are promoting "quality assurance" initiatives such as the various ISO certifications, but I think this needs to be said.

In case you are not familiar with it, "ISO" is the International Standards Organization, a voluntary federation of standards-setting bodies from around the world. They promote uniform ways of assuring quality output in many industries by documenting standards such as ISO 9000 and ISO 14001. Obtaining the certifications is expensive and time-consuming, and many consulting firms are making big money by pushing the standards.

When I receive a four page questionnaire from a customer asking how we comply with their ISO requirements, my first thought is not "How can I pass this off to someone else?" That just expands the "sabotage" into my organization. Assigning the questionnaire to someone else adds importance to the item which may not be deserved.

Instead, my first thought is, "Do I really need this customer?" I see that the last year's sales to this customer were less than $1,000 (and less than $200 the year before). The profit on that $1,000 was not enough to even justify taking the time to write back that we will not be filling out their form.

My action would be quite different for a larger and more important customer, of course. But I wonder how that small customer was talked into crippling their own ability to get good prices on products they need by establishing standards that are not in their own best interest. I would like to have that standards consultant's salesperson working for me – except that I would always wonder about their personal ethics.

And to the consultants making money from pushing those standards, I have a simple question. Do you ever tell your clients that they may encounter people like me who won't jump through their hoops and therefore cause them to lose a good source, all because of their "standards"?

Chapter 12
DEALING WITH PEOPLE AND HORSES

We have some horses just for fun and I've watched them for years because I'm interested in their behavior. Here is a quote attributed to the late Yogi Berra:

You can observe a lot just by watching.

The biggest thing that I have learned by watching horses and other animals is that they watch me while I'm watching them. They anticipate my movements based on what I've done in the past.

When I walk into the paddock and take candy out of my pocket for the horses, they learn to expect the same thing the next time I visit also. So I bring them candy – but only the first time that I visit them each day. I am completely consistent in this behavior and they generally ignore me on my second or third visit in a day.

I also make no sudden moves around the horses – ever – so they don't worry about me being near them when they're eating or when I'm filling the water trough. I'm completely predictable to them. They don't like the running water, but they'll drink water out of my hands because I have never splashed water in their faces.

Now think about people you deal with every day. Some of them you trust because they are predictable, and some you won't turn your back on. Which ones do you prefer to deal with? And which one do you think you should be?

There are people who think that other people are always out to get them: to offend them, to cause them more work, to take advantage of them. I assume that these are the horses who did have water splashed in their faces. All I can do is try not to add to their concerns and remind them of a logical principle called "Occam's Razor" (sometimes spelled "Ockham"). The shortest version I have seen is this:

The simplest explanation is the most likely.

The general idea is to remove complicated explanations, especially for behavior, and figure out what is the most likely cause of an event. For example, if I find hoof-prints behind the barn, it is possible that they were caused by a zebra that escaped from the zoo and was attracted by the hay we put out for the horses. It is possible, but it is not the simplest explanation. The simplest explanation is that our own horses made those hoof-prints.

Using the same logical principle, the person who thinks he or she is being singled out or targeted by the boss (assuming that the non-butthead boss is not indeed targeting the person) needs to consider this:

Most people really don't care enough about other people to go out of their way to purposely offend them. It's much more likely that they just weren't thinking.

See? The simplest explanation is the most likely.

Now if you're a butthead boss and you do treat people differently just because you can – and I've known butthead bosses like that – then you deserve whatever bad karma you collect from that behavior.

Believe me, what goes around comes around and I don't need to be the one who makes it come around, either: you've already spelled out that future for yourself.

The universe will find a way.

Yes, I have heard butthead bosses say right out loud that they can treat their help that way because they're the boss. All I can suggest is that you don't want to be that way. Your help, your horses, will follow you farther and longer. And you won't have to worry about turning your back on them either.

One more quick saying, and I don't think any additional comment is needed:

Everyone has value, even if it's just to

serve as a bad example.

Chapter 13
THE THREE ENVELOPES

This is an old story that I learned years ago, and I'm including it here just to be sure that it is preserved. If you've been in management, there is a good chance you are already familiar with it.

The new chief financial officer (CFO) is arriving at his office on the first day of work and runs into the outgoing CFO at the door. This is a bit uncomfortable for the new CFO, but the old CFO says, "Hey, no hard feelings. Jobs come and go. In fact, I've done you a little favor and left three envelopes in your pencil drawer. If you ever feel like you can't handle whatever is going on, open one of the envelopes."

The new CFO thanks him and goes about learning his new job, forgetting about the envelopes.

A year or so later, the Board of Directors calls on the CFO to attend a special meeting about the lack of profit in the most recent year and the failing labor negotiations.

The CFO is worried about how he should handle this meeting, and then he remembers the three envelopes. He looks in the pencil drawer and sure enough, there in the back of the drawer are three envelopes labeled "1", "2" and "3".

The CFO pulls out the first envelope and opens it. The note inside says, "Blame it all on your predecessor." He thinks it over and justifies it to himself because, after all, his predecessor has basically told him to do this.

So he goes to the Board meeting, blames everything on the old CFO, and the Board accepts his explanation.

Another couple of years go by, profits go up and down, up and down, and down and down. The CFO receives another invitation to a Board meeting. He remembers the envelopes and pulls out the second one. The note inside says simply, "Blame the economy."

Again the CFO takes the advice from the envelope and again the Board accepts his explanation.

Two more years go by. The unionized workers are out on strike, the company's main product has become obsolete, sources of raw materials have dried up – which is okay because sales have fallen to practically zero – and again the CFO receives an invitation to the Board meeting.

The CFO works late into the evening, trying to find a way to present the facts that show some kind of hope for the continued existence of the company. He tries multiple charts and graphs, and every attempt looks worse than the previous one. Finally, he remembers the envelope in the back of his pencil drawer.

Considering that the previous two envelopes did indeed save the day, he retrieves the envelope marked "3" and opens it with some trepidation.

Inside the envelope, he finds a note which says simply, "Prepare three envelopes."

CONCLUSION

I hope you enjoyed "Tease the Monkeys – a guide to non-buttheaded management." This book is also available on Kindle and as an audiobook on Audible.

We would like to hear your stories about the butt-headed bosses you have encountered for the next edition of this book.

Please email them to TeaseTheMonkeys@gmail.com. We can publish them anonymously or with whatever name you choose, just try not to get the guy in the next cubicle fired.

- Chris

www.ingramcontent.com/pod-product-compliance
Lightning Source LLC
Chambersburg PA
CBHW070858220526
45466CB00005B/2041